The Complete Incomplete Lyrics Of Deep Wilson

Jacob's Old Shoes

Published 2014 by Jacob's Old Shoes

Copyright © 2014 M & M Jerram

All lyrics copyright © 1986, 1987, 1988, 1989, 1990, 1991, 1992, 1993, 1994, 1995, 1996, 2006, 2007, 2008 & 2009 M & M Jerram.
Except lyrics to 'Atomic War' copyright © 1979 J, M & M Jerram, and lyrics to 'When Two Sane People Meet' copyright © 2007 E, M & M Jerram.

All rights reserved.

ISBN-13: 978 0953081332
ISBN-10: 0953081338

The Complete Incomplete Lyrics Of *Deep Wilson*

All 58 song lyrics from every album between 2006 and 2009

Plus more...

CONTENTS

A Thousand Ways
All The Ugly People
And I Walk
Aphids
Atomic War
Below The Lilies
Box Of Chocolates
Closed Again
Driving Back
Empty Bottle
For All The Reasons
Give 'Em Rice
Hide Away
Holes
Hong Kong '97 … Smile!
How Long?
I Want To Sail The Unknown Seas
I'm Going To Die
In Between In Love
In The Dark
It's All My Fault
It's Christmastime Once More
La Di Da And Birthdays
Letter In My Mind
Mine And Your Snow
Moonlight Sonata
My Mate John
My Wonderful Brain
Nag Nag Nag
No Harps, No Wings, No Pearly Gates
Pencil Drawing Man
Pity Little Men

Rampion
Sever
Sha La La Lucifer
Silence Me
Sinkfly
Small Distant Star
Something Of Nothing
Such Is Hope
The Better Angels
The Cover Version
The Girl Next Door
The Only One Of Me
There's No Answer
There's Something Special In A Smile
This Is Our Chance To Act Like Kids
Together Apart
Use Electricity
What She Was
When Two Sane People Meet
Where Cinderella Fell
Who Can Say
Without A Sound
You've Really Got To Go
Your Sunny Day
Zero
One More Song

Deep Wilson

A Thousand Ways

A name that I could say in a thousand ways
A name that I could write in a thousand lines
It's a shape forever written on my mind
And it is now or never, just before my eyes

The wings of the butterfly
The buzzing of the bee
The songs of the nightingale
Is reason for me to...

To stand on the mountains
Go swimming in the seas
To pray to the demigods
The name for me

A hand that I could hold in a thousand ways
A nose that I could blow for a thousand colds
Age is just a number for the very old
This is now our summer, as we slowly unfold

The wings of the butterfly
The buzzing of the bee
The songs of the nightingale
Is reason for me to...

To stand on the mountains
Go swimming in the seas
To pray to the demigods
The name for me

The wings of the butterfly
The buzzing of the bee
The songs of the nightingale
Is reason for me

To stand on the mountains
Go swimming in the seas
To pray to the demigods
The name for me

To stand on the mountains
Go swimming in the seas
To pray to the demigods
The name for me

(Laxton's Superb, 2007)

All The Ugly People

Why do I get my days mixed up
With all its never ending Tuesdays
And I don't know the number
Or how many have thirty-one
My times tables I've never learnt
Don't you just keep adding one
The alphabet confuses me
Free the letters ABC
Filing systems make me scream
With foreign tongues that frighten me
I want to be understood
I just want to be understood

My tears make me wet
My muscles make me weak
My bones make me mortal
My flesh makes me creep
My voice makes me dumb
My breath makes me choke
My tears make me wet
My muscles make me weak
My bones make me mortal
My memory I forget
My name makes me unknown
But I don't care

We are all the ugly people
And we, we are all we need to get by
We are all the ugly people
And we, we are all we need to get by
We're all the ugly people

Just don't let them take your dreams
We are all the ugly people
And we, we are all we need to get by

(Atomic Dolly, 2006)

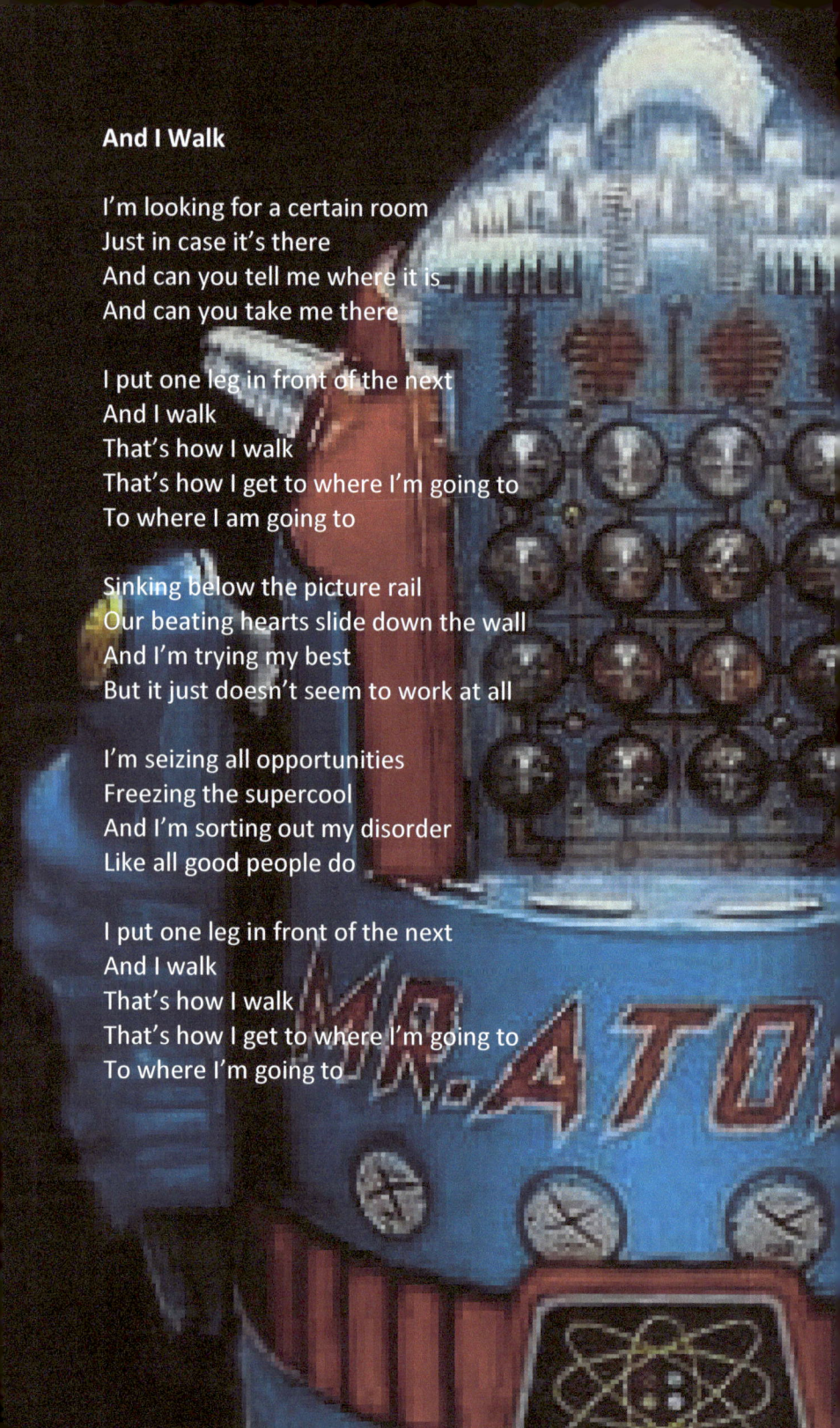

And I Walk

I'm looking for a certain room
Just in case it's there
And can you tell me where it is
And can you take me there

I put one leg in front of the next
And I walk
That's how I walk
That's how I get to where I'm going to
To where I am going to

Sinking below the picture rail
Our beating hearts slide down the wall
And I'm trying my best
But it just doesn't seem to work at all

I'm seizing all opportunities
Freezing the supercool
And I'm sorting out my disorder
Like all good people do

I put one leg in front of the next
And I walk
That's how I walk
That's how I get to where I'm going to
To where I'm going to

Citizens I give you
The beginnings of my boot
Lie down, face up
Close your eyes
If you want
If you want
If you want

(Atomic Dolly, 2006)

Aphids

I'm covered in aphids
Knee deep in screaming kids
I'm gonna blow my top, when will it stop
I'm covered in aphids

I've hoovered the carpet
Always cleaning someone's sick
I wanna read my book, it's something new
I'm covered in aphids

I'm covered in aphids
And they're milking me dry
Uncovered and naked
Believe me, I just want to cry
I'm covered in aphids
And they're bleeding me dry
Uncovered and naked
Thieving me of my time

Stinking like a mattress
Don't let the bed bugs bite
I wanna rest my head, think about sex
I'm covered in aphids

Unbutton my harness
Release me from my crimes
I'm gonna clear my name, write it out again
I'm covered in aphids

I'm covered in aphids
And they're milking me dry
Uncovered and naked
Believe me, I just want to cry
I'm covered in aphids
And they're bleeding me dry
Uncovered and naked
Thieving me of my time

I'm covered in aphids
And they're milking me dry
Uncovered and naked
Believe me, I really, really, really want to cry
I'm covered in aphids
And they're bleeding me dry
Uncovered and naked
Thieving me of my time

(Laxton's Superb, 2007)

Atomic War

After the Atomic War
Brrrrrrrr
There was nobody left
Except for me and my brother
And he was a bit of a big head

Atomic War
Atomic War
Atomic War
Atomic War
Atomic War

Everybody was thrown up, thrown up
Over the universe
There was blood on the ground
Mangled bodies all around
Didn't have a care
I was lying there bare
On my own
All alone
Except for me and my brother
Except for me and my brother

Atomic War
Atomic War
Atomic War
Atomic War
Atomic War

(A Box Of Chocolates - 20 Assorted Classics, 2006 & The Best Of The Sunday Songs, 2008)

2008

Dizzwah, UK: i do like this weeks sunday song. But me thinks i'm gonna come back and listen to it in the morning when i'm normal.

13. SINKFLY – 1992
Meikel, Germany: The meaning of life watched through the eyes of a fly and the buzzing at the end - very deep (wilson). ;)

14. EMPTY BOTTLE – 2007
Dizzwah, UK: im liking empty bottle. i got a few empty ones myself.. and a mega hangover to go with them

...N THE DARK – 1992
...phane Flowers, France: In The Dark ...eautiful...

16. ATOMIC WAR – circa 1980
...UK: ha ha ha ha ha ha ha, laugh? ...rly wet myself! I absolutely LOVE ...c war', what a brilliant 'tonic' for a ...day afternoon! So..the end of an era

---

Compilation m...
UNCLECHIMNEY MA...

All songs written & ...
M & M JERF...
Except
track 3 – Caleb ...
track 9 – Lennon/Mc...
track 12 – Jones/...

Copyright 2008 ZAXEY R...

ZAXCOMPS002

Mark & Martin would like to ... everyone who dropped by to ... listen!

Mark, USA: Sunday's will ne... the same. But thanks for al... previous ones.

Below The Lilies

Hold me near
Tell me love is here
Tell me nothing's to fear
Tell me all that I want to hear

Hold me close
Don't let me go
Don't let me fall
Please don't take me for a fool

And I'm
Below the lilies and the long hair
Pulled out from under the wheel
And I need to know how I feel
And I need to know what is real

(Laxton's Superb, 2007)

Deep Wilson

Box Of Chocolates

Everybody wants a box of chocolates
Not a picture of a flushing toilet
One of those with a fluffy kitten
Once shy, twice bitten
Like those men in their flying machines
I will clean up like Mr. Sheen
Mmm, yummy yummy
I've got love in my tummy
And I feel like stuffing me

Start on the hazel whirl
I'm told they make your teeth curl
And your breath smell
Never mind the postman's blind
Look at the coffee cream
Sitting there so serene
Shame it tastes like a sweaty rugby team

Next it's the orangy segment bit
Made to look like an orangy segment bit
But of course, it doesn't look like it a bit
'Cause it's brown
Throw it to the ground
Tell it to stay away
And don't come back another day

And you've got the fudgy one
The hudgy fudgy mudgy one
It sticks to your teeth
And it won't budgy one

Deep Wilson

Oh, there's the strawberry cream
Is this like the coffee cream
No, it's strawberry flavour
So pop it in
You start to grin
Until you hit the jammy bit
Ooh, the jammy bit
Oooh, the jammy bit
Yuk, out you spit
Then it hits the orangy segment bit
Which now looks like a doggy-do on the pavement

Oh, by the way
I forgot to tell you
I just love Turkish delights
That's why I ate them last night

What's that long one
It's the crickenal crunchy munchy
Pop that in
Half a way
And bite a bit
Oh, it flinters splinters
And cuts your throat
And you die

Goodbye

(A Box Of Chocolates - 20 Assorted Classics, 2006 & The Best Of The Sunday Songs, 2008)

Closed Again

All the rain is falling down
But I never see it hit the ground
The wind beats hard against my window
But I shut my ears, block out the sound

The walls of my room they are dripping
And the water runs down to the floor
My window frames they are rotting
But I just forget when I close the door

My absent mind forgets all the time
And I know my mind bets all the time
No-one has time for me anymore

But I can do it if I want to
Control it if I want to do
Make it if I need to
But once the feeling's there is gone
I look around and I just find a door closed again

I sit and fester in the darkness
I don't know how I find the time
Changing things with my eyes closed
And see my penance fit the crime

So could I find a new direction
One I haven't seen before
Lifts my heart for several minutes
And resurrects my aching core

My absent mind forgets all the time
And I know my mind bets all the time
No-one has time for me anymore

But I can do it if I want to
Control it if I want to do
Make it if I need to
But once the feeling's there is gone
I look around and I just find—

Do it if I want to
Control it if I want to do
Make it if I need to
But once the feeling's there is gone
I look around and I just find a door closed again

(In 1609 We Came Back To Earth, 2009)

Driving Back

Driving back through foggy weather
Radio on, more calm than ever
The mist closing in don't scare but comforts me

I'm thinking how things could be so different
Would it have changed if I'd been patient
The choices that I made then so long ago

You came along at a time in my life
No direction left or right
You came along and I wrote you a song
And now I know just where to go

Sometimes in my life thoughts come right back to me
Look at the past not as it could've been
Question myself my life and what I've done

I rely on the fact that I'll get over it
So what if one day I don't get over it
Could my spirits sink like the winter sun

You came along at a time in my life
No direction left or right
You came along and I wrote you a song
And now I know just where to go

(In 1609 We Came Back To Earth, 2009)

Deep Wilson

Empty Bottle

My window is stretched long and thin
Along the length of my bottle-neck
My face reminds me
Of something from Easter Island

No other faces around the neck
I place my thumb over the hole
Tip it up and water fills the gap
To remove my thumb is to see it flow

Water cascades with a rage
And the drain now takes the strain
I love, I love my empty bottle
But now I must remove the label

Reading the words it can't spell
From beginning to end gives me strength
I now know all it can tell
A thirst quenched, a life lost

Words cascade with a rage
And my brain now takes the strain
I love, I love my empty bottle
But now I must remove my label

(The Best Of The Sunday Songs, 2008)

Deep Wilson

For All The Reasons

I love it
For all the reasons
A day squeezed
With all the seasons

Let it manifest
Inside your head
Spread out its arms
Around your heart

The phoenix sings
Inside my car
It's in reverse
But never far

The heart in my chest
Beats like the rest
After butterflies
I start to cry

I've had an insight into what it was like
A taste of the world unknown to me
The coming together of the phoenix that sings
Makes me think what might have been

(A Box Of Chocolates - 20 Assorted Classics, 2006)

Deep Wilson

Give 'Em Rice

Throw the weighted dice
Who has the biggest slice?
Everything has its price
So go ahead and give 'em rice

Eating my TV dinner
I become a left winger
I become a gunslinger
I become a Top Of The Pops singer
I become a dead ringer
And I deserve it
'Cause I'm the breadwinner

Give 'em rice   (Sugar my tea)
I'm far too nice   (For what I see)
You've got to be cruel   (To be kind?)
I'm no fool   (But you're blind)

Throw the weighted dice
Who has the biggest slice?
Everything has its price
So go ahead and give 'em rice

Eating my TV dinner
I become a quiz show winner
I become an Olympic swimmer
I become Ethel Skinner
I become a 50s' R&R swinger
And I deserve it
'Cause I'm the breadwinner

Give 'em rice   (Sugar my tea)
I'm far too nice   (For what I see)
You've got to be cruel   (To be kind?)
I'm no fool   (But you're blind)

Throw the weighted dice
Who has the biggest slice?
Everything has its price
So go ahead and give 'em rice

(A Box Of Chocolates) 20 Assorted Classics, 2006

Hide Away

I look at myself
But is that me really there
I stick out my tongue
Scratch my unshaven hair

I open my mouth
And like the heat from a stove
Both my eyes melt
Boy, oh boy, do I need help

I made my head so I can hide in it
Hide away from everything
I made my bed so I can lie in it
Hide away from everything

I look for some time
The clock face stares back at me
I lick my thumb
And then I write my own name

'Cause it's always the same
Wondering who's really inside
Nothing changes
I just close my eyes.

I made my head so I can hide in it
Hide away from everything
I made my bed so I can lie in it
Hide away from everything

It's always the same
Wondering who's really inside
And then nothing changes
I just close my eyes.

'Cause I made my head so I can hide in it
Hide away from everything
I made my bed so I can lie in it
Hide away from everything

(Laxton's Superb, 2007)

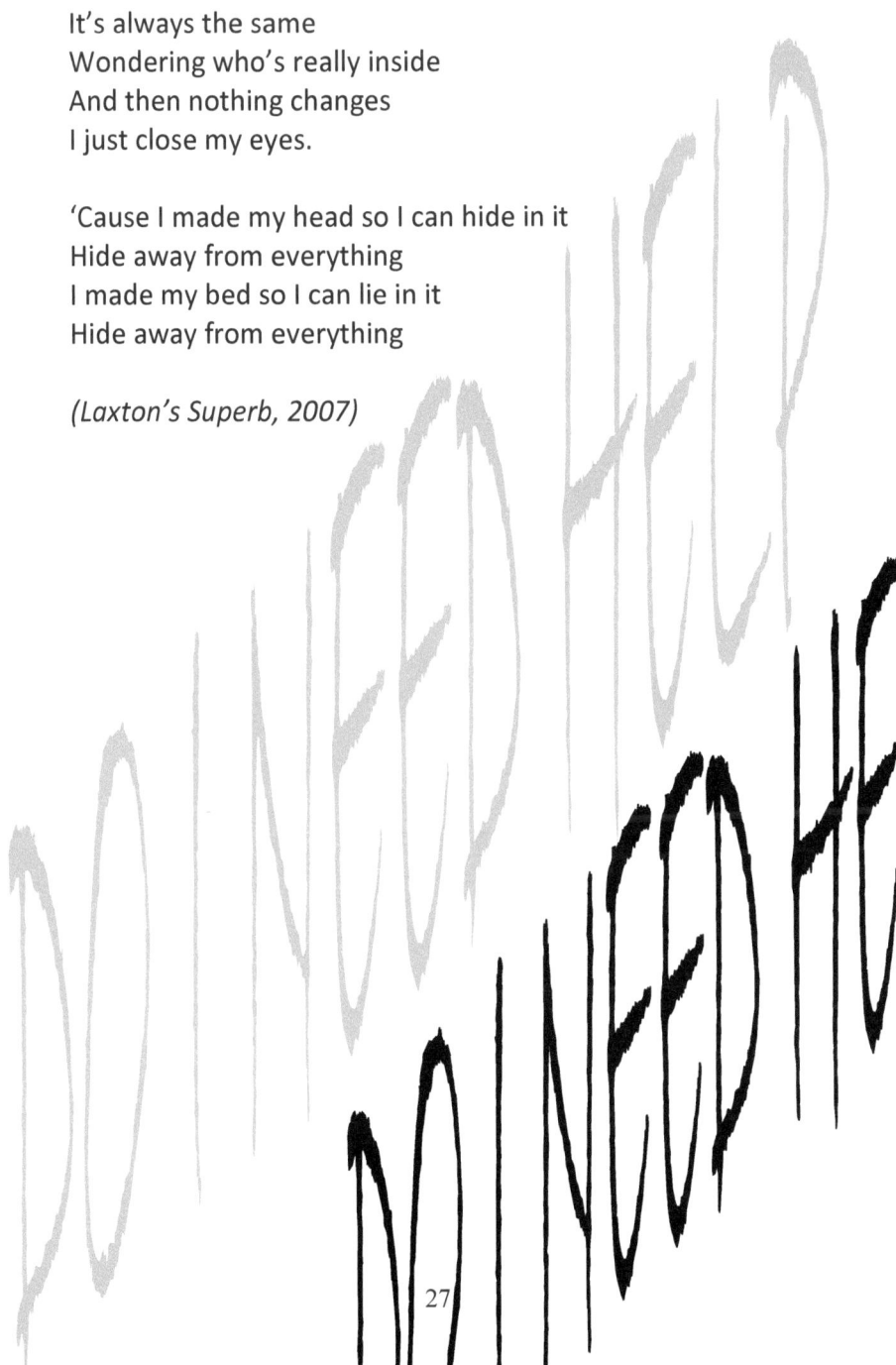

Holes

The cheese it has holes in it
The net it has holes in it
Everything has holes in it
That is just how it is

Apportion the blame equally
It's always the same can't you see
I've no-one to blame apart from me
And that's just how it is

Catapult the empty boat
  into the sea again
I wear that coat with all the holes
  out in the rain again

Like Vikings on a hovercraft
I'm sinking, I am sinking fast
Hold the oars close to the floor
And that's just how it is

There is no colour, there's no-one
There's no magic island in the sun
There's just carnage everywhere
And that's just how it is

Catapult the empty boat
  into the sea again
I wear that coat with all the holes
  out in the rain again

(Atomic Dolly, 2006)

Hong Kong '97 ... Smile!

I'm dead on my feet
As I walk these narrow streets
High-sided buildings dwarf me
To nothing much more

This is why I sing
This is the world dying
But I am still alive
Kicking inside your womb
Shedding the skin of time

I wrote to my friend
In good English I spelt it out
But she only spoke French
And nothing much more

This is why I sing
This is the world dying
But I am still alive
Kicking inside your womb
Shedding the skin of time

I have moved to the next room
Where I can see myself
In a mirror

This is why I sing
This is the world dying
But I am still alive
Kicking inside your womb
Shedding the skin of time

Nature threw life into my lap
And she thinks she can take it back
I should be the one to choose
I've got a brain I'm able to use

For every word you've ever said
There's twice as many in your head
And when you smell the smells you've smelled
You can't forget the lies they tell
So click your heals and nod your head
Believe in always what you said
But as you smile and look at me
I'll turn away and drop the key

Hong Kong '97 ... Smile!

(Atomic Dolly, 2006)

How Long?

I try and keep my hands busy
It isn't very easy
When you're cold and parts are freezing
My legs are weak
My arms are strong
There's nothing at my feet
No meaning to my song
There's no meat on my plate
No mouth to feed anyhow

How long?
In the dust I write it
I'm strong
In the hopes I carry

I try to keep my mind busy
It isn't very easy
When you're old and keep on sleeping
I'm shut up here within these walls
Alone with all my fears
So formidable and tall
I start to tear down
The paper covering the walls

How long?
In the dust I write it
I'm strong
In the hopes I carry

(In 1609 We Came Back To Earth, 2009)

I Want To Sail The Unknown Seas

I want to sail the unknown seas
In a boat made from tall, dark trees
And I want to see the mountains move
And whole great continents too

With migrations
The world's in motion
With one changing face
Can't match the pace
Changes all the same
It's time to act its age

I want to leave gravity behind
In a rocket not of these times
And I want to see the stars explode
And whole great galaxies too

Only people
With new abilities
Need to have belief
And with all these people
At our disposal
There's nothing that can't be reached

I want to sail the unknown seas
In a boat made from tall, dark trees
And I want to see the mountains move
And whole great continents too

Only people
With new abilities
Need to have belief
And with all these people
At our disposal
There's nothing that can't be reached

I want to sail the unknown seas

(Laxton's Superb, 2007)

I'm Going To Die

Shaving foam behind my ear
Misshapen and insincere
I attract dirty looks
I try hard but it never works

Such a fine head of hair
Black blanket cut into squares
I cough till my lungs rip
Silverfish are laughing in the sink

I'm going to die
This is the end
I struggle with my bones
Like out-of-control controls

I'm in a spin
I'm in a nose-dive
Panic then steps in
Wearing shit stained jeans

My cornflakes know how to swim
But this battle I'm gonna win
Calmly I dim the lights
And push all of them out of sight

Objects contort in front of me
Losing their shape, capacity
I'm bereft of all my thoughts
My stomach is tied in double knots

I'm going to die
This is the end
I struggle with my bones
Like out-of-control controls

I'm in a spin
I'm in a nose-dive
Panic then steps in
Wearing shit stained jeans

(A Box Of Chocolates - 20 Assorted Classics, 2006 & The Best Of The Sunday Songs, 2008)

In Between In Love

The sun has shone on me today
Hit me with its ultra violet rays
It was just how I wanted it to be
Laying down so unexpectantly

While basking in the sun's own heat
I didn't know what was in store for me
Now my head is spinning in a daze
And my heart it shimmers in the haze

I've got that feeling in my skin
That feeling of living
Short grass around
Long grass I tread
I yearn to find that flower bed

The grass is green
The sky is blue
I am in between in love with you

I see a bud so fresh and new
In the whole of my panoramic view
The flower opens up in front of me
To reveal itself in its full glory

Her eyes they begin to glisten
As her ears pick up and listen
To the bird on the branch above us sing
To the tune that she wrote only just last spring

I've got that feeling in my skin
That feeling of living
I look above
And I look below
And I look at us from head to toe

The grass is green
The sky is blue
I am in between in love with you

(A Box Of Chocolates - 20 Assorted Classics, 2006 & The Best Of The Sunday Songs, 2008)

In The Dark

As lights go out
I hear noises of the night
On nerve endings they bite
I want to scream out loud

My mind expands
To fill the empty room
And perhaps beyond
Unsettling dust

I haven't got a clue
I haven't got an idea
Totally in the dark
Hiding in my fear
I haven't got a hope
I haven't got no trust
And another thing
I think I think too much

As I open my eyes
They feel the touch of darkness
Pawing at my eyes
Deriding my blindness

I put out my hands
As if to break my fall
I collapse inwards
And swallow it all

I haven't got a clue
I haven't got an idea
Totally in the dark
Hiding in my fear
I haven't got a hope
I haven't got no trust
And another thing
I think I think too much

(A Box Of Chocolates - 20 Assorted Classics, 2006 & The Best Of The Sunday Songs, 2008)

The Complete Incomplete Lyrics Of

It's All My Fault

How could you do that to me
I'm sitting here all alone
You were not real
No real friend to me
Just like someone you've never known

I know what you're thinking
And I know what you are going to do
I watch you when I'm dreaming
Lying in the arms of someone new

But when I see you again
It makes me feel all right
See you up inside my head
Come alive
It just cannot be my fault
That it went oh so wrong
I think it is
I know it is
I think I know it's all my fault

But when I see you again
It makes me feel all right
See you up inside my head
Come alive
It just cannot be my fault
That it went oh so wrong
I think it is
And I know it is
I think I know it's all my fault

(In 1609 We Came Back To Earth, 2009)

It's Christmastime Once More

It's that time, time of year
To forget all your troubles
And just, just remember
It's Christmastime once more

Merry Christmas, merry Christmas
Everybody's having fun
Snow's falling
Reindeers calling
It's time to have a ball
Bells ringing
Children singing
It's Christmastime for all

Santa Claus is leaving Lapland
Santa Claus is on his way
Snowmen will come to life
For this very special day

Merry Christmas, merry Christmas
Everybody's having fun
Snow's falling
Reindeers calling
It's time to have a ball
Bells ringing
Children singing
It's Christmastime for all

Hanging up the Christmas tree lights
Hanging up the tinsel
Sitting in front of the fire
You start to sing and whistle

Hanging up the mistletoe
Hanging up the holly
Waiting for a kiss or two
While you're warm with Molly

Merry Christmas, merry Christmas
Everybody's having fun
Snow's falling
Reindeers calling
It's time to have a ball
Bells ringing
Children singing
It's Christmastime for all

Merry Christmas, merry Christmas
Everybody's having fun
Snow's falling
Santa's calling
It's time to have a ball
Bells ringing
Children singing
It's Christmastime for all

(A Box Of Chocolates - 20 Assorted Classics, 2006)

La Di Da And Birthdays

Sweep the pavement round the bench
There tonight she'll lay her head
People passing, heading home
No time to stop and say hello

Little voices
Little things
Little voices
Sing, sing, sing

La di da and birthdays
La di da and always
The fag machine's taken her money and run
She'll never see her maladjusted son
La di da and birthdays
La di da and always

Now the ghosts are on her feet
Cold seeps in and takes her seat
Hair of long forgotten thoughts
Old rag shoes, yesterday's news

Little voices
Little things
Little voices
Sing, sing, sing

La di da and birthdays
La di da and always
The fag machine's taken her money and run
She'll never see her maladjusted son
La di da and birthdays
La di da and always

La di da and birthdays
La di da and always
The fag machine's taken her money and run
And she'll never see her maladjusted son
La di da and birthdays
La di da and always

Shadows falling across her eyes
No-one sings her auld lang syne

(Atomic Dolly, 2006)

Letter In My Mind

There's a letter in my mind
And that letter is P
P for Peter paid Paul
To rob Mary from me

There's a letter in my mind
And that letter is A
A for Adam ate an apple
No matter what you say

We play games to pass the time
We learn the rules once in a while
Turn of a card
And the throw of a dice
Decisions we learn to live by
Decisions we learn to live by

There's a letter in my mind
And that letter is I
I for an eye, and a tooth for a tooth
We're all gonna die

There's a letter in my mind
And that letter is N
N for nothing never no-one
Finally it's amen

We play games to pass the time
We learn the rules just once in a while
Turn of a card
And the throw of a dice
Decisions we learn to live by
Decisions we learn to live by

We play games to pass the time
We learn the rules just once in a while
Toss of a coin
The blink of an eye
But our actions are what we decide
Our actions are what we decide

(Laxton's Superb, 2007)

Mine And Your Snow

I shadow box around your room
Trying to find what I haven't lost
The window sill on which I lean
Is cold to touch, it makes me ill

I've blurry visions of many things
My eyes' distortion eclipses it
But drifting on the southern winds
Is all the oxygen we could ever need

Don't wrestle yourself from me
Please breathe in slowly with me
I've lost the reflex to let go
Cos I know this is mine and your snow
This is mine and your snow
This is mine and your snow
And you're a thought away from home
And I'm a dream away from living
This is mine and your snow
This is mine and your snow

And you're a thought away from home
And I'm a dream away from living
This is mine and your snow
This is mine and your snow
This is mine and your snow

(In 1609 We Came Back To Earth, 2009)

Deep Wilson

Moonlight Sonata

It's a moonlight sonata
Broken in the gutter
Who wrote I love you
Forever on the wall

Every waking hour
Every sleepless night
I'm thinking so much of you
And what you were always like

Life is short and the gods they are against you
I'm a genie looking for its next meal
Life is short and the heavens are above you
So stand by my side
Don't leave me behind

In fears I'm a wealthy man
Collecting tears in a can
And when I have to
I'll rain them down on you

My surroundings enclose me
My heart starts to race
I can see all the danger
Where the streets are never straight

Life is short and the gods they're all against you
I'm a genie looking for its next meal
Life is short and the heavens are above you
So stand by my side
Don't leave me behind

Life is short and the gods they're all against you
I'm a genie looking for its next meal
Life is too short and the heavens are all above you
So stand by my side
Please don't leave me behind

(Laxton's Superb, 2007)

My Mate John

Life's been treating me hard
And I've been waiting around
For someone to give me a hand
And help me from the ground

Well people walk over me
Treading me into the dirt
I'm digging a hole and hiding
But soon I'll come out fighting

When my mate John gets here
You'll all be sorry
'Cause he's the driver of a ten ton lorry
He's ten feet tall and six feet wide
And remember please, he's on my side

You may stand there and laugh
But I will have the last laugh
'Cause soon my turn will come
When this worm begins to turn

'Cause when my mate John gets here
You'll all be sorry
'Cause he's the driver of a ten ton lorry
He's ten feet tall and six feet wide
And remember please, he's on my side

(A Box Of Chocolates - 20 Assorted Classics, 2006)

Deep Wilson

My Wonderful Brain

The girl in the blue dress
Was a blur
I saw an elbow
But nothing more

There is a bubble
Going around
Above their heads
I've heard it said

I'd like to kill
All of the violence
And the sun on the hills
Gives me the kind of thrill

To be alive
With

My wonderful brain
Have you got one the same
Evolution's been heading this way
And I don't think things will ever be the same with

My wonderful brain
Have you got one the same
Evolution's been heading this way
And I don't think things will be the same

My wonderful brain
Have you got one the same
Evolution's been heading this way
And I don't think things will ever be the same with

My wonderful brain
Have you got one the same
Evolution's been heading this way
And I don't think things will be the same anymore
I don't think things will be the same anymore
I don't think things will be the same, oh yeah
I don't think things will be the same

(Atomic Dolly, 2006)

Nag Nag Nag

You were a breath of fresh air
In my dull and pointless life
I was in love without a care

You were such sweetness and light
I was helpless, I couldn't fight
It was just good to be alive

But now you're always on my back
Nag nag nag nag
Always in my ear
Nag nag nag nag nag nag
I can't escape your naaag
I can't escape your nagging

There was nothing I wouldn't give
You used to be dear to me
But now you're just so expensive

It was first do this then do that
You even made me comb out my hair
And that is something I can't forgive

But now you're always on my back
Nag nag nag nag
Always in my ear
Nag nag nag nag nag nag
I can't escape your naaag
I can't escape your nagging

I can't suffer this you bitch
I'll keep the car, you can have the kid

But now you're always on my back
Nag nag nag nag
Always in my ear
Nag nag fucking nag
I can't escape your naaag
I can't escape your naaag
I can't escape your nagging

(A Box Of Chocolates - 20 Assorted Classics, 2006 & The Best Of The Sunday Songs, 2008)

The Complete Incomplete Lyrics Of

No Harps, No Wings, No Pearly Gates

Well you'll find no harps, no wings, no pearly gates,
  no fluffy clouds or swirling mist
We just spend the whole time getting pissed

It may come as a shock
That I sniff my socks
That's just how I am
And I like showing who is boss
Henry the 8th with a Bernard Burger
And Beethoven with a triangle
I've made Karl Marx an H2 Owner
And Van Gogh watch Paint With Nancy
There's Adam without any clothes
And Dickens with a quill up his nose

Oh God, what have you done
Humiliation for everyone
Oh God, what have you done
You've made a bad world for everyone

Oh dear me, slap my face
I've put the universe in disgrace
I guess now it goes without saying
That there's no need in praying

Marilyn under a Groucho mask
Chopin playing a stylophone
Rodin moulding plasticine
Anne Boleyn with a neck scarf
Elvis with an aspirin
Rasputin with a water-ring

Deep Wilson

Oh God, what have you done
Humiliation for everyone
Oh God, what have you done
You've made a bad world for everyone

I have these two big buttons
One's good and one is bad
They are colour coded
One is red and the other is red
Oh no, I'm seeing double
Oh man, are you in trouble
I've had one too many kegs
And I think it must have gone to my head

Oh God, what have you done
Humiliation for everyone
Oh God

(A Box Of Chocolates - 20 Assorted Classics, 2006)

Pencil Drawing Man

I'm a pencil drawing about to be rubbed out
There's nothing to do, I can't even shout
Without having a speech bubble next to me
Hey brothers, let's liberate, be free

I lose my legs
I lose my arms
I lose my mind
I lose my charms
Completely erased
Rubber bludgeoned to death
I believe I've nothing left

I gain my body
I gain my legs
I gain my arms
I gain my head
Completely restored
Scribbled with love to life
Which I won't give up without a fight

I gain some wood
I gain some rope
I gain a noose
I think I'm to lose
Completely dazed
I'm hung by the neck
Until I'm nothing but dead

I'm a pencil drawing about to be rubbed out
There's nothing to do, I can't even shout
Without having a speech bubble next to me
Hey brothers, let's liberate, be free

(A Box Of Chocolates - 20 Assorted Classics, 2006 & The Best Of The Sunday Songs, 2008)

The Complete Incomplete Lyrics Of

Pity Little Men

Pity little men in a crowd
Such a feeling they arouse
Under attack of the mockingbirds
Poor cows with binoculars

And when I'd say is your toupee straight away
   you'd say go away good day

You're really indifferent
Insignificant to me you'd be
You're one of many
A penny in a bank
Of copper you stank
One row in a rank
You toe the line
Wasting time
Facing death
Preparing
Rehearsing
Cursing the day you die
And I'll be there to say goodbye

Pity little men in a crowd
Such a feeling they arouse
Under attack of the mockingbirds
Poor cows with binoculars

And when I cry under what sheets you lie
   through your teeth to me not he

There's really no point
No Sunday joint, in me carrying on
You're so very wrong
You're gone to the world
It's easy to tell
Coins in a wishing well
You throw them in
Hear nothing
Looking down
Stopping
Waiting
That empty hole
Your empty life
With no goal

Pity little men in a crowd
Such a feeling they arouse
Under attack of the mockingbirds
Poor cows with binoculars

(A Box Of Chocolates - 20 Assorted Classics, 2006)

Rampion

As I walk through the forest
I don't see a soul
Pushing aside the foliage
My body feels the cold
I'm looking at the roses
In their many tens
Choosing a few of the best
To leave behind the stems

She caught my eye, and blinded me
She caught my eye
I had to let the roses fall
I had to let the roses fall

So I'm lost in this forest
I don't know where I am
I think I'm gonna die here
I think I might as well die here
I enter a clearing
A tower looms high
And there at a window
A face to banish night

She caught my eye, and blinded me
She caught my eye
I had to let the roses fall
I had to let the roses fall

But there is no door
And there are no stairs
Why don't you lean out
And to let down your hair

She caught my eye, and blinded me
She caught my eye
I had to let the roses fall
I had to let the roses fall

I had to let the roses fall
I had to let the roses fall

(In 1609 We Came Back To Earth, 2009)

Sever

I wash my hair
But it doesn't seem
To make the grass grow
So, I don't know

I fill my boots
With all of the food that I grew
Out in the field
So, there you go

Sever all links
Weather all seasons
I'm really into
Finding a reason

Sever all links
Weather all seasons

I burnt a hole
Straight through my torso
But it didn't bleed
No, not a bit

Holding my nose
I lick these overalls
Over dinner
So, is that it?

Deep Wilson

Sever all links
Weather all seasons
I'm really into
Finding a reason

Sever all links
Weather all seasons

(A Box Of Chocolates - 20 Assorted Classics, 2006)

Sha La La Lucifer

Always read between the lines
All the blank spaces filling up your mind
Beware of the devil in fine detail
Yell, rebel, let's create hell

Pablo Diablo are you the one
I've sold your daughter, killed your only son
I'm doing many things I cannot tell
And I'm not stopping for anyone
Oh, I am not stopping for anyone

So sha la la lucifer
I'm ready to explode
Sha la la Lucifer
I really feel the cold
I really feel the cold

The devil's in me, it's gonna be fun
Satan can whisper his merry song
I've waited too long, I can't ignore
The shoulder on which I carry her

I need her germs to multiply
All the bacteria I have inside
If this is hell then give me more
Fire and brimstone, bring in on
Oh, fire and brimstone, bring it on

Sha la la lucifer
I'm ready to explode
Sha la la Lucifer
I really feel the cold
I really feel the cold

So sha la la lucifer
I'm ready to explode
Sha la la Lucifer
I really feel the cold
I really feel the cold
I really feel the cold

(Laxton's Superb, 2007)

Silence Me

Working from the inside
I'm trying to get out
I've worn my fingers to the bone
And I'm all out of shout

I'm going round in circles
Round and round and round
I've got no tread left on my shoes
And my head it starts to pound

I must calm down
Compose myself
After all that's been said
I hate myself
Please silence me
Stop these lips
First with a finger
And then with a kiss

I'm no ordinary sinner
A beacon of the night
I feel so silly when I speak
I've set myself alight

The sky it blackens over
It's looking just like rain
Let me settle on the ground
To try once again

I must calm down
Compose myself
After all that's been said
I hate myself
Please silence me
Stop these lips
First with a finger
And then with a kiss

I must calm down
Compose myself
After all that's been said
I really hate myself
Please silence me
Stop these lips
First with a finger
And then with a kiss

(Laxton's Superb, 2007)

Sinkfly

If I ask you a question
Will you tell me no lies
If I ask you for hope
Will you look me in the eyes

Why, why, why, why, why am I a sinkfly
Why, why, why, why, why am I a sinkfly
My life revolves around the sink
Continually avoiding the drink
Why, why, why, why, why am I a sinkfly
I hope there's more when I die
I hope there's more when I die

I propagate my own kind
Into a world that I despise
I try and stay alive
Even though I want to die

Why, why, why, why, why am I a sinkfly
Why, why, why, why, why am I a sinkfly
My life revolves around the sink
Continually avoiding the drink
Why, why, why, why, why, why am I a sinkfly
I hope there's more when I die
I hope there's more when I die
When I die

(The Best Of The Sunday Songs, 2008)

THE BEST OF THE SUNDAY SONGS!

November 2007 – July 2008

1. I'M GOING TO DIE – 1995
Diana, USA: I love I'm going to die..it epitomizes Deep Wilson...great lyrics and presentation..fantastic spacey instrumentals..each note planned perfectly..a complete song that doesn't leave you hanging..its pure enjoyment! I [c]ould have a cd of just this song and play [it] over and over.

2. NAG NAG NAG – 1991
[Glo]ria, UK: another good 'un lads!! nowt wrong with a bit of punk on a sunday evening!!

[3.] YOUR PHRASING IS BAD –

[4. I]N BETWEEN IN LOVE – 1991
[..., A]ustralia: First to Listen - Music [..]'s with the vocals (sorry - Lol) [...]ed second time (same haha)

[5. ...]PE – 1992
[... r]elaxing!!! =)

6. PENCIL [...]
Rina, Italy: oh [...]

7. THE GIRL NEXT [DOOR]
Annette, Australia: Hi [...] There - Don't Move An[...] Right Back at Lunch Ti[me...]

8. WHAT SHE WAS (DEMO) – 200[?]
Virginia, USA: Hi I listen to your Sun[day] song. And of course I listened to it tw[ice I] think it's a beautiful song...

9. PAPERBACK WRITER – 20[??]
Mozelle, USA: YES WAAYYYY!!! dee[p] wilson's "paperback writer" ROCKS!!...

10. BOX OF CHOCOLATES – 1988
Sarah, UK: aaaah ha ha ha ha brilliant!!! love it! so reminiscent of Viv Stanshall....& with the Clangers on backing vocals! genius! loads of love guys xxxx (:>

11. FUME
Victoria, UK: i love your sunday songs....perfect way to start the day!!!

Small Distant Star

As the sun finally sets
And the sky loses its red
I look straight above
Looking for the one I love
I'm held in the darkness
Feeling tense and perplexed
There's one and then two
Until finally it's you

That small distant star
I just can't take my eyes from
It stares back at me
A distance that's far too long

So few notice your shine
Unaware you're even there
They worship the sun
Obvious people everywhere
As you ignite the skies
With the flames of hell
I want to hold you
As you fall in on yourself

That small distant star
I just can't take my eyes from
It stares back at me
A distance that's far too long

(1994 version : A Box Of Chocolates - 20 Assorted Classics, 2006)
(2009 version : In 1609 We Came Back To Earth, 2009)

A Box Of Chocolates

20 Assorted Classics

Something Of Nothing

Sometimes I feel so small
I swear I don't exist at all
Go on brush me aside
And carry on with your life

Sometimes I close my eyes
And watch the shadows passing by
I then open my eyes
And the darkness strikes me blind

I'm crap
I'm no good
A waste of space
Born to lose
Put me down
Something of nothing
Something of nothing

I think of big numbers
Lay them in a line like counters
Sometimes when I reach six
I feel my brain strain and split

I look all around me
And nothing at all attracts to me
I feel I'm at the centre
Of the expanding universe

I'm crap
I'm no good
A waste of space
Born to lose
Put me down
Something of nothing
Something of nothing

(A Box Of Chocolates - 20 Assorted Classics, 2006)

Such Is Hope

Look around
It's not so good
Should we keep on
With keeping on
With unknown endeavour
Where does it hide
Secrets
That can be found

Reaching out
Touching the stars
The meaning of life
With open eyes
Like three blind mice
Once etched in time
Now holding
The carving knife

Such is hope
Heaven's own gift
To struggling mortals
Pervading
Like some subtle essence
From the skies
All things
Both good and bad

Lost so much
Had so little
You drop to your knees
Conceding
But there's always a spark
There inside
Stand up
It waits for you

Such is hope
Heaven's own gift
To struggling mortals
Pervading
Like some subtle essence
From the skies
All things
Both good and bad

(1992 version : The Best Of The Sunday Songs, 2008)
(2009 version : In 1609 We Came Back To Earth, 2009)

The Better Angels

Her palms are red
Her fingers spread
Something's got
Inside her head

Soft fine lines
Clear blue eyes
But she can't
Make up her mind

I've just seen the better angels
Approaching from the fold
I've just seen the better angels
Spilling chosen colours in the road

An abrasive thing
To commit a sin
But now it's time
Unclip your wings

The sky is high
No sense of time
We all fall down
Like the nursery rhyme

I've just seen the better angels
Approaching from the fold
I've just seen the better angels
Spilling chosen colours in the road

(Atomic Dolly, 2006)

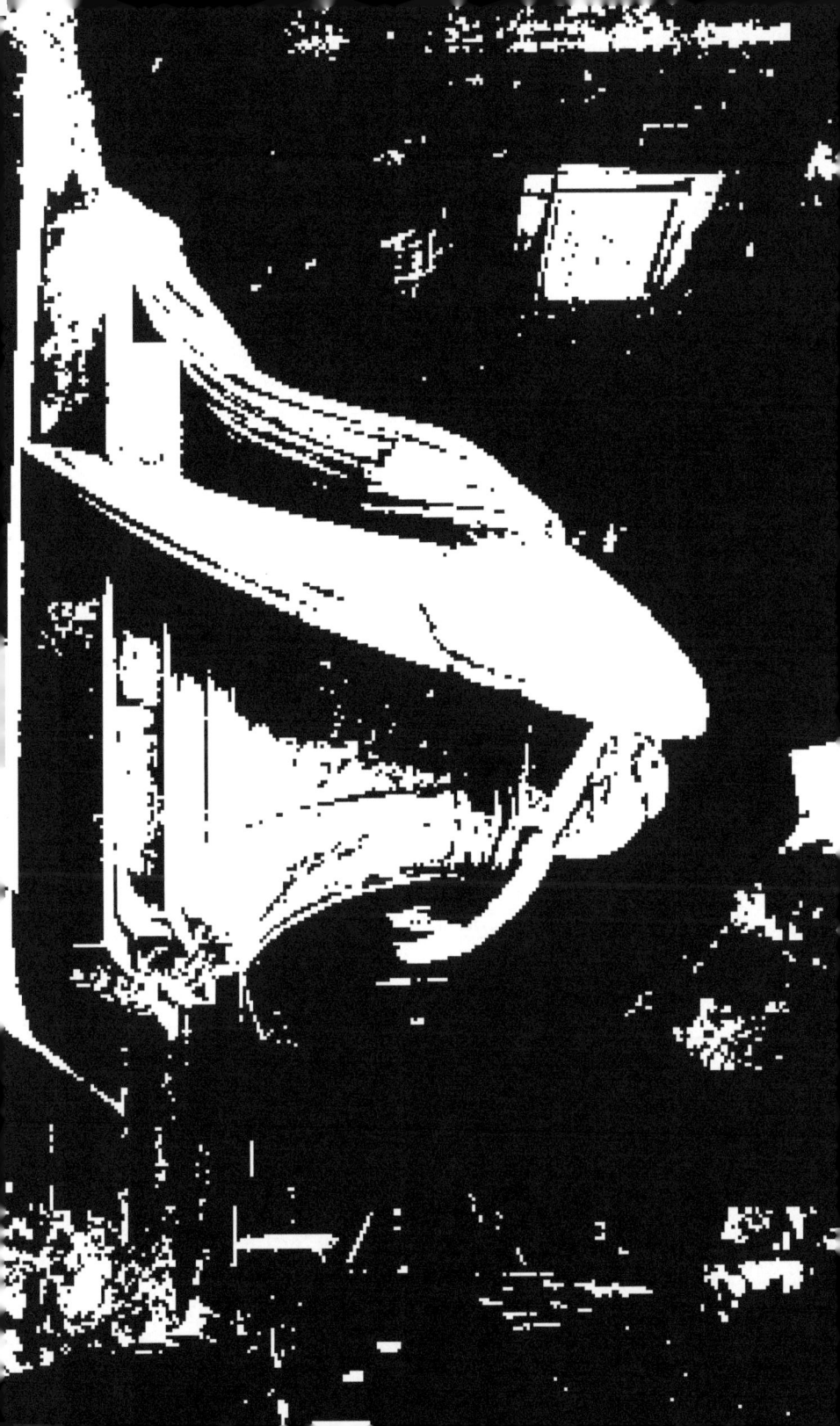

The Complete Incomplete Lyrics Of

The Cover Version

Everybody's doing a bland new thing now
Come on baby, do the cover version
I know you'll get to like it if you give it a chance now
Come on baby, do the cover version
Pete Waterman told me you can do it with ease
It's easier to learn than your ABCs
So come on, come on, do the cover version with me

I just can't, I just can't
I just can't control my bowels
Neither can, neither can
Neither can our oldest fan
They look so happy
When they've filled their nappy
With a load of crappy
Such a big fun Chappie
I just can't, I just can't
I just can't control my bowels
Neither can, neither can
Neither can our oldest fan

Take, Take, Take, Take, T-t-t-t-take, Take...
Take or leave us
Only please believe us
She is always gonna be disababled
The producers have reduced us
Into nothing more than inflatables
Inflatables, Inflatables...
At the end of the day
We can honestly say
That we have always been drugged up to the eyeballs
Take, Take, Take, Take, T-t-t-t-take, Take us away, Way

There's too many drongo songs in the world
And most of them done by Stock Aitken & Waterman
Dags and dropkicks are everywhere
But I want R— H—

Two little boys called Matt and Luke
Bought a stylophone with all their loot
But they couldn't play it as good
As R—, my favourite Aussie

This may be the saddest song
Written by Stock Aitken Waterman
It's about two Liverpudlian girls
Who said they wanted to jack
But they got the sack
But they got the sack

They said they would do anything
Rock and Roll and even Fleetwood Mac
But then Sonia came along
And stabbed those poor girls in the back
She stabbed them in the back
She stabbed them in the back

But you'll never stop me stabbing the lot
If you're gonna keep me from my No.1 spot
You'll never stop me from my No.1 spot
Oh oh oh oh
Never stop, stop, stop
My No.1 spot
Spot

(A Box Of Chocolates - 20 Assorted Classics, 2006)

The Girl Next Door

The girl next door's
Impaled on the school railings
She's screaming rather loud
But she looks so enchanting
So enchanting
Yeah she looks so enchanting
You know the girl next door
On the school railings
She looks so enchanting

The kids crowd round
And they sit and start watching
The teachers make their sounds
And ask her where it's hurting
Where it's hurting
The teachers make their sounds
The teachers make their sounds
And ask her where it's hurting

They say, stay right there
Don't move an inch
Stick a finger in her eye
Does she flinch
I've got the flair
I've got the tender loving care
I don't know why
It always makes them cry

The girl next door's
Impaled on the school railings
She's screaming rather loud
But she looks so enchanting

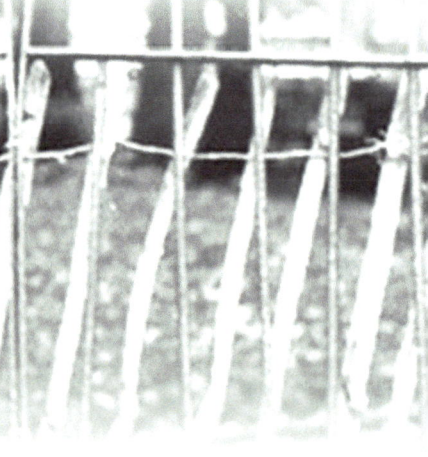

So enchanting
Yeah she looks so enchanting
You know the girl next door
On the school railings
She looks so enchanting

After a little thought
I guessed she was just faking
And though it may sound cruel
The railings I started shaking
Started shaking
The railings I started shaking
And though it may sound cruel
Yes, the railings I started shaking

They say, stay right there
Don't move an inch
Stick a finger in her eye
Does she flinch
I've got the flair
Got the tender loving care
I don't know why
It always makes them cry

I bet her mother's proud
Of her little girl
She's drawing such a crowd
Shame about the curls
Shame about her
Shame about her curls
I bet her mother's proud
But it's a shame about her curls

She says, stay right there
Don't move an inch
Stick a finger in her eye
Does she flinch
I've got the flair
Got the tender loving care
I don't know why
It always makes them cry

(A Box Of Chocolates - 20 Assorted Classics, 2006 & The Best Of The Sunday Songs, 2008)

Deep Wilson

The Only One Of Me

Once upon a time in a land far away
There lived a man who looked just like me
He wore my clothes and he spoke just like me
He stole my shoes and then used my name

I poked him in the eye 'til we cried, 'til we cried
I punched him once for luck, but I knew I had to stop

So why can't I be the only one of me
Is it too much to ask in this age of us
And why can't I be the only thing you see
Is it too much to ask, but I do, I must

I turned the other cheek, but he mirrored me
I held out my best hand, but he raised me three
He's in my mind, crazy and insane
And if I close my eyes, he's there all the same

So why can't I be the only one of me
Is it too much to ask in this age of us
And why can't I be the only thing you see
Is it too much to ask, but I do, I must

He's in my mind, both crazy and insane
And if I close my eyes, he's there all the same
I poked him in the eye 'til we cried, 'til we cried
I punched him once for luck, but I knew I had to stop

So why can't I be the only one of me
Is it too much to ask in this age of us
And why can't I be the only thing you see
Is it too much to ask, but I do, I must

(In 1609 We Came Back To earth, 2009)

There's No Answer

I'm standing angels over trains
Shaping Playdoh in your name
Nothing changes
It all stays the same

I had a ticket in my hand
A fine and delicate little plan
But what I saw, I couldn't say
I had no reason why

But how can something be so wrong
When it feels so right
And how could we stand there and laugh
When we felt so sad
I know there's no answer
But I can't help but wonder
What might've been

I'm holding handfuls of the rain
Trying to keep myself so sane
But all mixed up and all confused
Lying thinking of you

I need to fix my broken mouth
Stop me chewing collarbones
It wasn't me - It never is
Just some crazy hope

Deep Wilson

But how can something be so wrong
When it feels so right
And how could we stand there and laugh
When we felt so sad
I know there's no answer
But I can't help but wonder
What might've been

And how, and how, and how can something be so wrong
When it feels so right
And how could we stand there and laugh
When we felt so sad
I know there's no answer
But I can't help but wonder
What might have been

(Laxton's Superb, 2007)

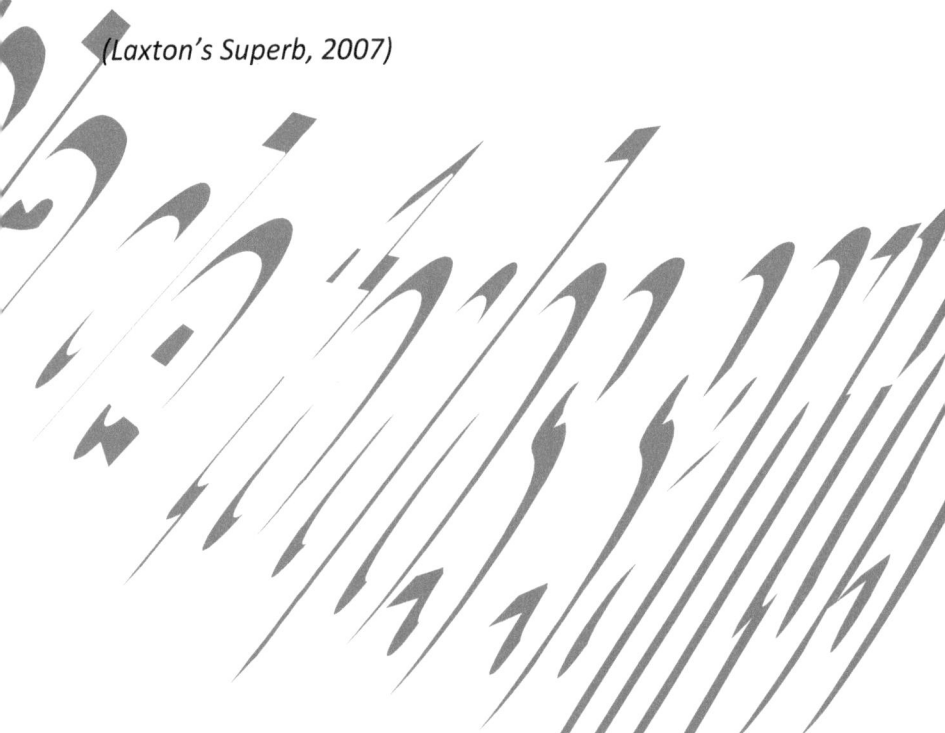

There's Something Special In A Smile

The nights are getting longer
The p'licemen are getting younger
But I'm just sitting here getting older

The world is getting madder
The people are getting sadder
But there's one thing that makes us happy
Every one of us

There's something special in a smile
Something special in a smile
Something special
Something special
Something special in a smile

Wars are always raging
And disasters always hap'ning
So why can't people see what they're facing

If your waters are always murky
And your grandad's a Christmas turkey
Then you shouldn't worry
I'm not that hungry

There's something special in a smile
Something special in a smile
Something special
Something special
Something special in a smile

If you're no-longer a spring chicken
And you see no use in wishing
Then all I can say to you
Is have a Kipling

There's something special in a Kipling
Something special in a Kipling
Something special
Something special
Something special in a Kipling

There's something special in a smile
Something special in a smile
Something special
Something special
Something special in a smile

(A Box Of Chocolates - 20 Assorted Classics, 2006)

This Is Our Chance To Act Like Kids

This is our chance to act like kids
Run around and dance and skid
Dressing up to make believe
This is how it's meant to be

This is our chance to raid the fridge
Eat everything until we're sick
I'm a clown miming sounds
You're an upright lady lying—

Come on won't you just dance with me
Across the floor to lock the door
Come on won't you pretend with me
Who is you and who is me

This is our chance to act like kids
Being like we never did
With chewing gum in your hair
And coco-pops flying everywhere

This is our chance to raid the fridge
Eat everything until we're sick
I'm a clown miming sounds
You're an upright lady lying—

Come on won't you just dance with me
Across the floor to lock the door
Come on won't you pretend with me
Who is you and who is me

(Laxton's Superb, 2007)

Together Apart

See - my cold stare
Just staring - into air
See - your reflection
Does it scare you - that I'm here

You know you won't win
Mad man's knowing grin
I won't bat an eyelid
Not one facial twitch

So hear my laugh
Together apart

I - will not bite
As long - as I've just been fed
I'm - in a cage
Where I sit - I sit and I day-dream

Opening up the mail
Cut and fold set sail
In a phone box
Speaking to the clocks

So hear my laugh
Together apart
So hear my laugh
Together apart

(Atomic Dolly, 2006)

Use Electricity

I'm invisible - I'm hidden
I'm in the undergrowth - But listen
All is quiet - All is cold
So hear the secret - To be told

Plug it in now
Flick the switch
You're now connected
To the National Grid
It's written on the roof
For everyone to see

All is dark - And all is cold
And I'm divisible - By seven
All is quiet - All is calm
But now it's time - To raise the alarm

Plug it in now
Flick the switch
You're now connected
To the National Grid
It's written on the roof
For everyone to see

Everybody use electricity
It's written on the roof
For every one two three

Plug it in now
Flick the switch
You're now connected
To the National Grid
It's written on the roof
For everyone to see

I'm invisible - I'm hidden
I'm in the undergrowth - But listen
All is dark - And all is cold
So hear the secret - To be told

Plug it in now
Flick the switch
You're now connected
To the National Grid
It's written on the roof
For everyone to see

(Atomic Dolly, 2006)

What She Was

She couldn't been seen from the moon
But I saw her enter the room
And thousands of people stood in the way
But I, I could only see one thing

Her hands raised up to the sky
Her feet about an inch from the floor
And she dabbled in tricks and things of the mind
Who can say what she was

What she was
Was what she was
And what she wasn't
Wasn't enough to know
What she was
Was what she was
And what she wasn't
Just goes to show
Just goes to show

She's surely the last of her kind
And I'm, I'm going out of my mind
Holding the stars and the planets too
I just seem to want to cry

I wish I had a magic word
A secret smile or a clever tattoo
Then I could unleash from the world
And holiday on the moon

What she was
Was what she was
And what she wasn't
Wasn't enough to know
What she was
Was what she was
And what she wasn't
Just goes to show
Just goes to show

(Demo Version : The Best Of The Sunday Songs, 2008)
(Final Version : In 1609 We Came Back To Earth, 2009)

When Two Sane People Meet

This is the day of our lives
A day that we can celebrate the things
That mean so much to us
A future that spreads out its wings
And flies in the face of fear
Unhappiness can wear its happy face
For a change my friend
Is just about the same as me

And when two sane people meet
And finally standing in the same two feet
They just know
And when two sane people meet
The crazy world can run around and spin
On its head

This is the time of our lives
A time we mustn't hesitate to bring
The X-men to our party
Batman 'n' Robin should come too
The Silver Surfer's eating cake
I don't know why he didn't think to thank me
Just Super Heroes with nothing too much else to do

So when two sane people meet
And standing finally in the same two feet
They just know
And when two sane people meet
The crazy world can run around and spin
On its head

Deep Wilson

When two sane people meet
And standing finally in the same two feet
They just know
And when two sane people meet
The crazy world can run around and spin
On its head

This is the day of our lives
A day that we can celebrate the things
That mean so much to us
A future that spreads out its wings
And flies

(Laxton's Superb, 2007)

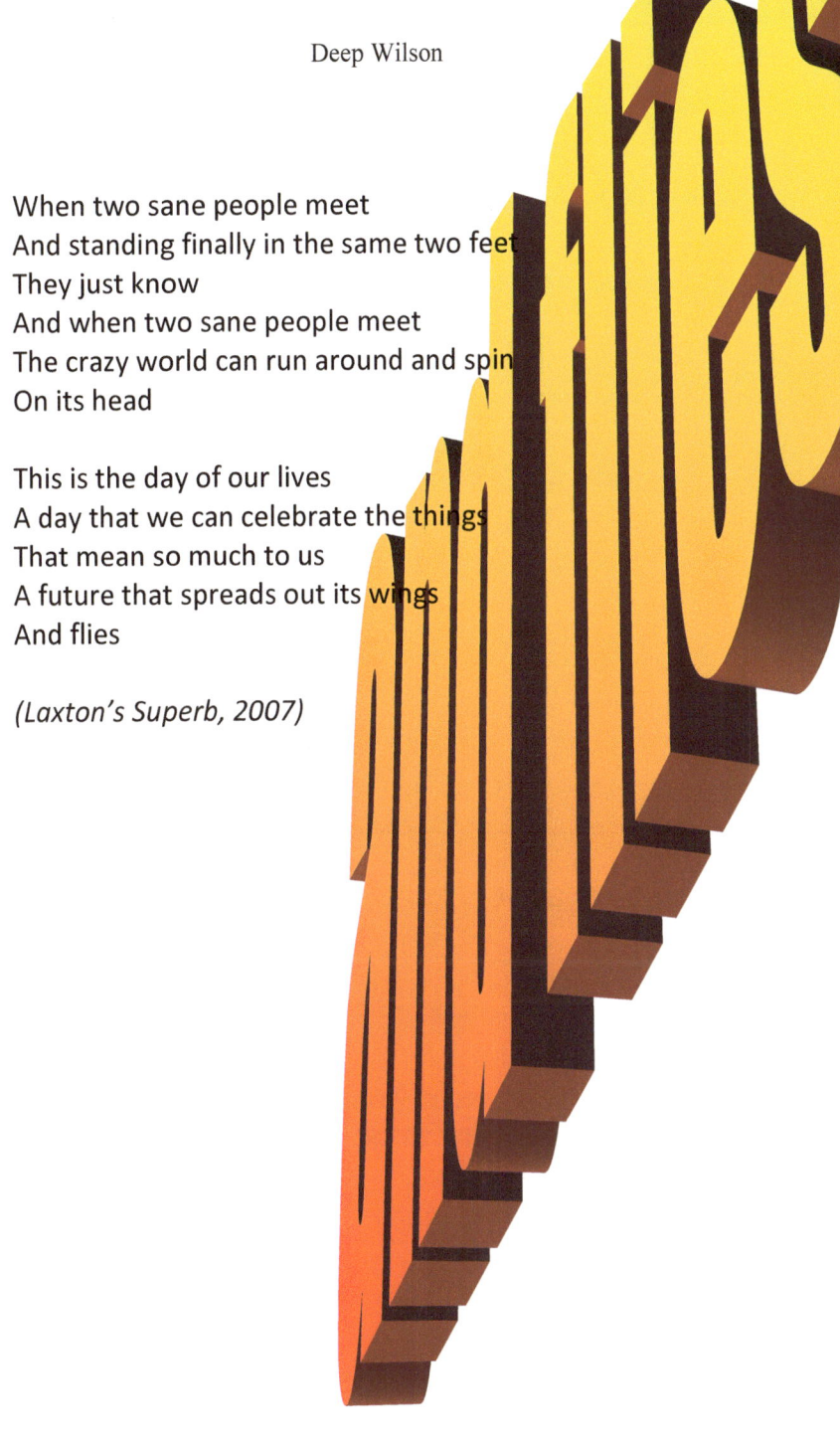

Where Cinderella Fell

I'm moved by your legs
I dance about, dance, dance around, dance
You spill your head
Around the golden calf I dance

I'm standing where Cinderella fell
I'm standing where you created hell
I feel your pain in my head
I feel my hairs standing up on end

The ground could open up
And the devil smile with both hands cupped
But rivers flow
Which hold all my thoughts and hopes

I'm standing where Cinderella fell
I'm standing where you created hell
I feel your pain in my head
I feel my hairs standing up on end

I don't want to break up your happy home
But if I leave my number will you phone?

I'm standing where Cinderella fell
I'm standing where you created hell
I feel your pain in my head
I feel my hairs standing up on end

(Laxton's Superb, 2007)

Who Can Say

I'm looking out over mountains and streams
I am dusting off forgotten dreams
And who could say when I lost my way
But I won't let the decades drift away

And who can say if I did wrong
Was I nothing till you came along
Care free
Are we the same as you and me
But where would I be if you hadn't arrived
Would I thrived or even stayed alive
You could ask the same questions of me

Now I'm getting back to how things were before
But I don't know if I want it anymore
Maybe something has gone
Or has something gone wrong with me
Always has and will always be

But who can tell if I did wrong
Have I ever felt that I belong
Right here
But I think it's where I want to be
I know I sometimes seem to change my mind
Should've found myself a new pastime
But life ain't got a lifetime guarantee

But who can say if I've ever been right
Who can say I made your future look bright
With me
But I think it's where I want to be
If I could only have you by my side

It may even be a bumpy ride
Have faith in the things you cannot see

I'm looking out over mountains and streams
I am dusting off forgotten dreams
It may be too late but I do not care
We'll share
The next best thing to being there

(In 1609 We Came Back to Earth, 2009)

Without A Sound

In my veins - I felt a breeze
On my neck - On my knees
Empty space - Fills my head
Outside that - Is nothing else

I want to take everything in
Slowly take everything in
Today I felt a wrenching in my spine
A clenching in my side
I fell to the ground
Silently, without a sound

Are they blue? - I wish I knew
I think they are - But I can't be sure
Above that - A knot of hair
I can't make - The metal stairs

I want to take everything in
Slowly take everything in
Today I felt a wrenching in my spine
A clenching in my side
I fell to the ground
Silently, without a sound

(Atomic Dolly, 2006)

You've Really Got To Go

How could you
Employ me to be more than just your friend
As I'm struggling
Struggling with the end
How could you
Implore me to
You know this really has to end
But you're wanting
Wanting to make amends

But now you've really got to go
You know you look quite cute
But you stink of Brüt
And that discharge from your nose
Don't look too safe

But then again
You've got lots of go
In your high-heel shoes
And your three-piece suit
But do I really want to see you
Do I really want to see you
Do I really want to see you again

Well now you've really got to go
You know you look quite cute
But you stink of Brüt
And that discharge from your nose
Don't look too safe

Deep Wilson

Yet again
You've got lots of go
In your high-heel shoes
And your three-piece suit
But do I really want to see you
Do I really want to see you
Do I really want to see you again

Do I really want to see you
Do I really want to see you
Do I really want to see you again

(Laxton's Superb, 2007)

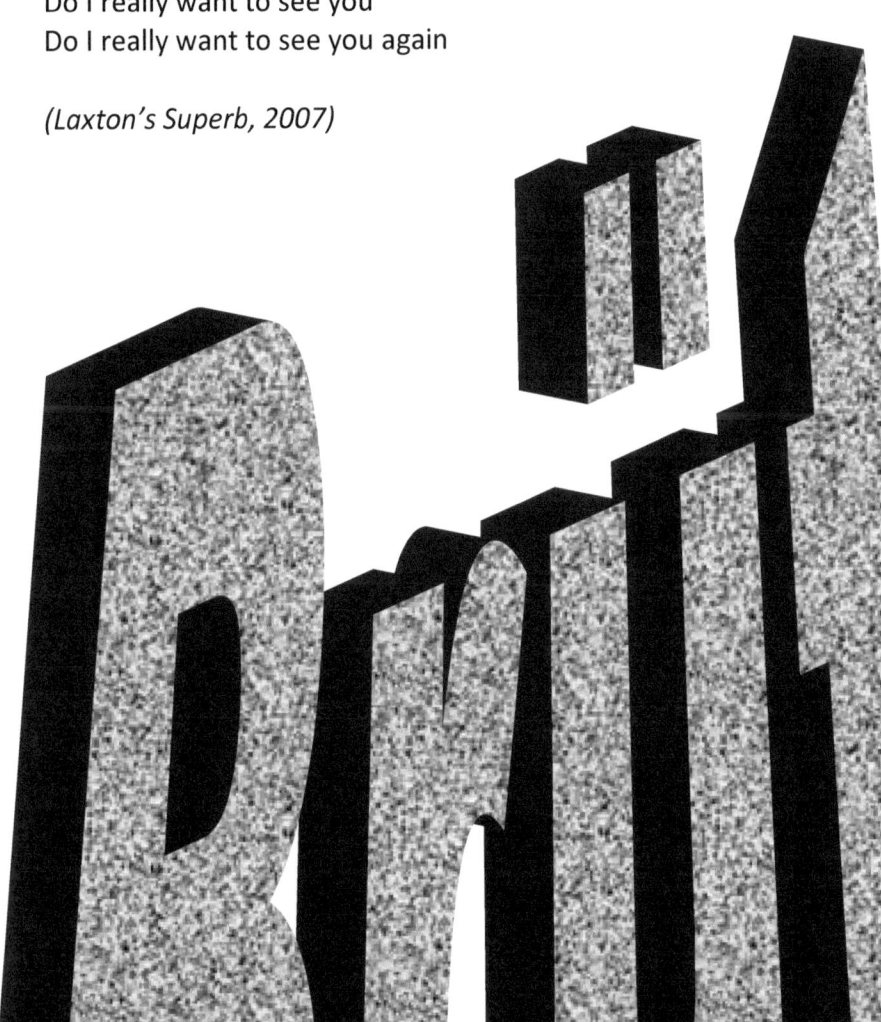

Your Sunny Day

Big red sun hanging in the sky
You made your way from morning 'til night
Now evening sings gentle on my ears
And the stars shine brightest on happy tears

The times we spoke
The times we laughed
The times we needed nothing to say
The times we did
The times we didn't
The times when only shadows played
I want to dream away your sunny day

I want to dream away your sunny day
Float upstream and fly away
I want to dream away your sunny day
Close my eyes and slow replay
I want to dream away your sunny day

Big red sun hanging in the sky
You watched over me and I thank you for that
But now it's time for us to sleep
Curl up tight and let our minds run free

I want to dream away your sunny day
Float upstream and fly away
I want to dream away your sunny day
Close my eyes and slow replay
I want to dream away your sunny day

(Atomic Dolly, 2006)

Zero

I rub my arm along the glass
It's smooth to touch - I've heard it hurts
Warm the water of a cold bath
I give my all - I give my soul

There's wine upon my lips
And ambrosia between my teeth
But tomorrow will be zero
As I become my own hero

This is the last song
This is the last song
Place your hands over your ears
Before the last song
This is the last song
This is the last song
Place your hands over your ears
Before the last song has gone

I'm in the bathroom - I'm downstairs
I'm not laughing - Cause I'm so upset
I've got a scab just like New Zealand
Just itching, itching on my skin

So I'm so full of shit
And my breath starts to stink
But tomorrow will be zero
Yes tomorrow will be zero
As I become my own hero

Peep Wilson

This is the last song
This is the last song
Place your hands over your ears
Before the last song
This is the last song
This is the last song
Place your hands over your ears
Before the last song is gone

(Atomic Dolly, 2006)

One More Song

What about one more song before we go

Just one more song and then we head for home

One more song is all I know

I wish I'd brought my Stylophone

What about one   What about one

One more song before we go

One more song before we go. Yeah, yeah, yeah

One more song before we go

(Atomic Dolly, 2006)

CAVE IN SPAIN

12/11/2006

Such sophisticated, simple folk
Connected well, how well they spoke
All communicating, eating lunch
Selecting, the best pick of the bunch

But cavemen walk amongst us now
Standing tall, shorter than the rest
With briefcase and bowler hats
Budget for inheritance tax

Your antecedents
Built your monuments
They built your success
Built your testaments
Built your nest eggs
And all because
We made love in a cave in Spain
We made love in the pouring rain
But we didn't believe in the stories told
Just made fire when the nights were cold
We made love in a cave in Spain
We made love in the pouring rain
But we didn't make war on a German shore
Or die slowly at Andorran heights

Such sophisticated, simple folk
Connected well, how well they spoke
All communicating, eating lunch
Dissecting, he knows a joke

Neanderthal, you are so droll
Who went and stole your ancestral home
Maybe/You're not quite the troglodyte
But show your face you look all right

June 2008

...of common touch
Looking for a grain of sand
Or one foreign alien hand

Maybe chorus or just extra bit or leave out.
I'm not sure how the story goes
Can you count on your fingers
All ten toes
I'm not sure you want to know the score
If I told you a little, You'd just want...

The Complete Incomplete Lyrics Of

Deep Wilson

Notes, Ideas and Doodles

Notes, Ideas and Doodles

Notes, Ideas and Doodles

Notes, Ideas and Doodles

Notes, Ideas and Doodles

Notes, Ideas and Doodles

Notes, Ideas and Doodles

Notes, Ideas and Doodles

www.ingramcontent.com/pod-product-compliance
Lightning Source LLC
Chambersburg PA
CBHW042335150426
43195CB00001B/1